Forgiveness
And Other Life Seasonings

Forgiveness
And Other Life Seasonings

Cathy Burnham Martin

Published and printed in the United States of America

www.QTPublishing.com

Quiet Thunder Publishing
Naples, FL   Manchester, NH   Columbus, NC

This title and more can be found at
www.GoodLiving123.com

<u>Dedication</u>

I humbly dedicate "Forgiveness: and Other Life Seasonings" to everyone who continues to work to keep compassion front and center in the midst of our complicated daily lives. Developing forgiveness skills is never easy but always worthwhile.

Sensitivity and empathy come very naturally to some people and yet not at all to others. Thank you for seeking and practicing forgiveness and compassion in your heart, mind, and spirit. By doing so, you not only generously sprinkle one of the most powerful Life Seasonings, but you serve forgiveness up with kindness and a sincere desire to alleviate suffering

May your abundance of this compelling ability lift you up in even the most challenging circumstances. Thank you again. God bless you.

Cathy

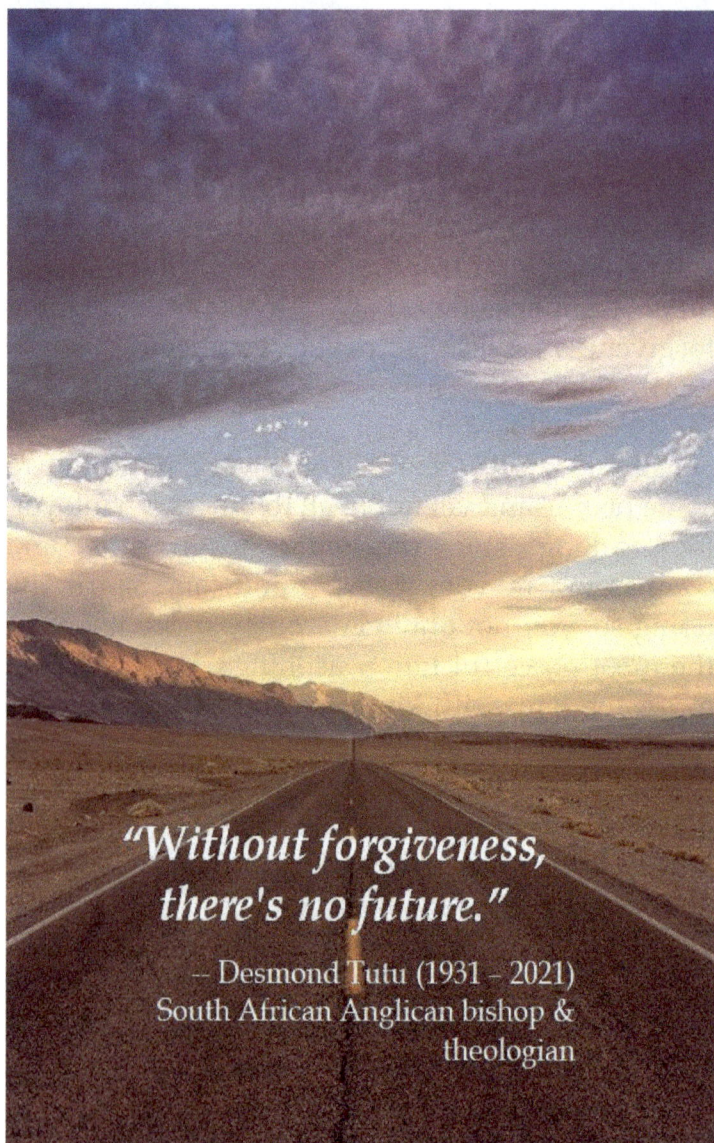

"Without forgiveness, there's no future."

– Desmond Tutu (1931 – 2021)
South African Anglican bishop &
theologian

<u>Foreword</u>

Many people hold a misconception that I live some sort of magically "charmed" life. They do not know of my personal struggles and challenges. I try not to wear suffering on my sleeve, so to speak. However, I do know the pain. I have been "done wrong." Like most of us, I have suffered multiple offenses. I have had to learn forgiveness.

> *"Anger begets more anger, and forgiveness and love lead to more forgiveness and love."*

> —Mahavira (either 6th or 5th Century BC)
> (also known as Vardhamana)
> 24th Tirthankara of Jainism

When a close family member did the family an injustice, the pain was horrible for me. He changed my life. People were shocked that he would steal from me and do so with such callousness. Many said he was motivated by his long-held jealousy of me. Some said he may have needed the money. I figured he had something to prove, most likely to himself. So be it.

He chose his insecurities and money over family. I was saddened to learn it could happen in my family. Why? Did I somehow think we were exempt? Silly me.

Regardless, I chose to not let his evil actions ruin my life. I forgave him. I turned the page. We cannot change the past.

My husband could hardly believe that I could forgive this relative. It was not as hard as I had imagined. I did my soul searching. I prayed. I let it go. And... I let him go.

"He that cannot forgive others
breaks the bridge
over which he must pass himself;
for every man has need to be forgiven."

-- Thomas Fuller (1608 – 1661)
English churchman & historian

Forgiveness is not always easy. In fact, it is likely never easy. But we need to forgive each other so the pain inflicted on us doesn't eat away at our happiness, our calm, our state of well-being.

Forgiveness is a vital Life Seasoning. And it is one we all need. We all can do this.

Table of Contents

(Photo by Adrien Moureaux)

<u>What It Means</u>

*"It's one of the greatest gifts
you can give yourself, to forgive.
Forgive everybody."*

-- Maya Angelou (1928 – 2014)
American memoirist, poet & civil rights activist

Psychologists study forgiveness as part of our healing process. It demonstrates personal growth.

Philosophically speaking, forgiveness is linked to justice and morality. It plays a powerful role in our interpersonal relationships.

In all religions, forgiveness is emphasized. There is both divine and interpersonal forgiveness.

*"Forgiveness is the fragrance
that the violet sheds
on the heel that has crushed it."*

-- Mark Twain (1835 – 1910)
(pen name of Samuel Langhorn Clemens)
American writer & humorist

(Photo by Alex Shute)

We may believe that we need to forgive others because the Bible tells us so. Jesus is noted for teaching that we should forgive others as God forgives us. Still, forgiving can be easier said than done.

When we forgive someone, it is not just words. We cannot simply say that we forgive someone. Forgiveness is a worthy process because it sets us free from pain, bitterness, and resentment. These are completely natural and normal feelings.

"Forgiveness is the economy of the heart...
forgiveness saves the expense of anger,
the cost of hatred, the waste of spirits."

-- Hannah More (1745 – 1833)
English religious writer & philanthropist

Letting go of our rightful position that we were wronged is difficult. However, if we hang onto the injustice committed against us, we have not forgiven.

Forgiving someone is not a passive act. Forgiveness is an active choice.

"Forgiveness really is so misunderstood,
as well as the power
it can release in an individual."

-- Jennifer O'Neill (1948 -)
Brazilian American model, author & actress

We need to forgive so no desire for payback can evolve. We must have no desire for revenge or retribution.

One of the difficulties in forgiving someone is that victims rightfully have strong feelings of betrayal. When we get blindsided, we tend to believe that forgiveness condones the behavior that harmed us. This is not true. We have vulnerabilities, and it hurts us deeply when someone takes advantage of us and treats us poorly.

(Photo by Stacey Franco)

*"When you forgive,
you in no way change the past –
but you sure do change the future."*

-- Bernard Meltzer (1916 – 1998)
American radio host

Some people believe that the offender must face consequences and even admit their errors before forgiveness can be considered. This is not true. We do not even have to tell the offender that we've forgiven them. They may never apologize anyway. Many offenders stubbornly cling to a false sense of self-righteousness.

"In order to have understanding,
you need forgiveness,
compassion, and empathy."

-- Rooney Mara (1985 -)
American actress

Further, some actions, such as betrayal, abuse, and severe trauma, can be extremely tough to forgive. This is especially true when the offender shows absolutely no remorse.

They have pride and may use it to build a wall around themselves. No matter how transparent, this is an attempt to feel disconnected from any and all responsibility for the harm that was caused. I mean, they were right, after all, right? Yeahhhh. Not so much.

"The ability to forgive is one of man's greatest achievements."

-- Bryant H. McGill (1969 -)
American poet, author & activist

(Photo by Shah Rokh)

Human Frailty

Forgive, not because you are weak, but because you are strong enough to understand that people make mistakes. We are stronger than we may seem.

(Photo by Mathew Schwartz)

*"The lesson is
that you can still make mistakes
and be forgiven."*

-- Robert Downey, Jr. (1965 -)
American actor & producer

On social media, I observed a friend sharing some personal pain. His posting simply said, "I never faked my care for anyone. If I stopped caring, it's because I found out that you weren't worth it."

Just a posting that is obviously filled with pain, frustration, and anger from betrayal.

Person B commented as a "friend." "It's more like you never really cared at all. If you are able to disengage so easily, it's doubtful that genuine caring existed."

(Photo by Juan Pablo Rodriguez)

My friend replied, "I see. So, what you're saying is after putting up with and giving a lot of care to an individual who just treated me like sh*t, stole all my money, and betrayed me, that if I stop giving them my help, it means I never really cared about the to begin with?"

To that, Person B said: "No, it means if they treated you like sh*t, stole your money, and betrayed you… and you didn't have a clue or were in denial about their treatment toward you, I would ask you why did you continue to remain in any type of relationship with them? The truth usually is you were getting something from them that kept you in the cycle of abuse. Normal people don't allow others to treat them that way."

My friend now crumbled into: "Ahh… got it… you're right. Thank you."

(Photo by Pablo Merchán Montes)

Arrrrgh. This sort of exchange infuriates me. We are not shrinks. We cannot understand the depth of our own issues, never mind someone else's. My friend needed support, not a slap 'up the side of the face.'

So, I tried to calmly express thoughtfulness and compassion with my reply. "It's hard to believe and then harder still to process betrayal, never mind when it's repeated. We stay because we continue to forgive. What we fail to often recognize is that the offender feels no sorrow nor need to repent. Our pain. Their loss. Try not to be so hard on yourself."

"I struggle with insecurities.
I struggle with forgiveness.
I struggle with letting someone go
that did me dirty without vengeance,
which is an evil thing."

-- Jessie Reyez (1991 -)
Canadian singer-songwriter

Personally, I do not recommend using social media to share wretched feelings. History shows that there are too many people who will attack, especially when someone is down or expressing differently than someone else thinks is "right."

(Photo by Natalia Blauth)

We can open our hearts to our nearest, dearest friends, of course. We are in this world to support each other. However, on social media, we can opt to only send our struggles to specific friends via private messaging, rather than blast posting for the world to see.

"Let us not listen to those
who think we ought to be
angry with our enemies,
and who believe this to be great and manly.
Nothing is so praiseworthy,
nothing so clearly shows a great and noble soul,
as clemency and readiness to forgive."

-- Marcus Tullius Cicero (106 BC – 43 BC)
Roman statesman, lawyer & philosopher

Try not to fear that forgiving someone may be misconstrued as condoning or excusing the wrongdoing. It is natural to want to rectify or make right the wrong that was committed. It can be very difficult to let go of resentment.

(Photo by Semenay Erdogan)

"Holding on to anger, resentment and hurt only gives you tense muscles, a headache and a sore jaw from clenching your teeth. Forgiveness gives you back the laughter and the lightness in your life."

-- Joan Lunden (1950 -)
American journalist, author & television host

*"To err is human;
to forgive, divine."*

-- Alexander Pope (1688 – 1744)
English poet

(Photo by Daniel Mirlea)

When we are trying to forgive someone, we need good self-care. We need compassion for both the offender and us. We can find extra strength by connecting with trusted friends and family. We all need a strong support system, especially in painfully trying times.

(Photo by Adam Nemeroff)

We always benefit when we learn to be kind to ourselves. Other people's needs often, if not usually, get put first. Sometimes, we must remind ourselves that if we don't keep ourselves renewed and refreshed, we will have less energy and strength to help others.

"Our lack of forgiveness makes us hate,
and our lack of compassion
makes us hard-hearted.
Pride in our hearts makes us resentful
and keeps our memory in a
constant whirlwind of passion and self-pity."

-- Mother Mary Angelica (1923 – 2016)
American Catholic nun

Another important tool to apply when we are dealing with our human frailty is challenging the negative around us. There is so much pessimism outside, and we get bombarded with cynicism by the news and social media. We need to block out the contradictions, neutralize the dissentions, challenge our own negative self-talk, and seek positive affirmations daily.

(Photo by Danila Balashkin)

"Selfishness must always be forgiven
you know,
because there is no hope of a cure."

-- Jane Austen (1775 – 1817)
English novelist

We grow when we are patient with ourselves, too.
Healing takes time. We can try to live calmly in the
present while building a positive future.

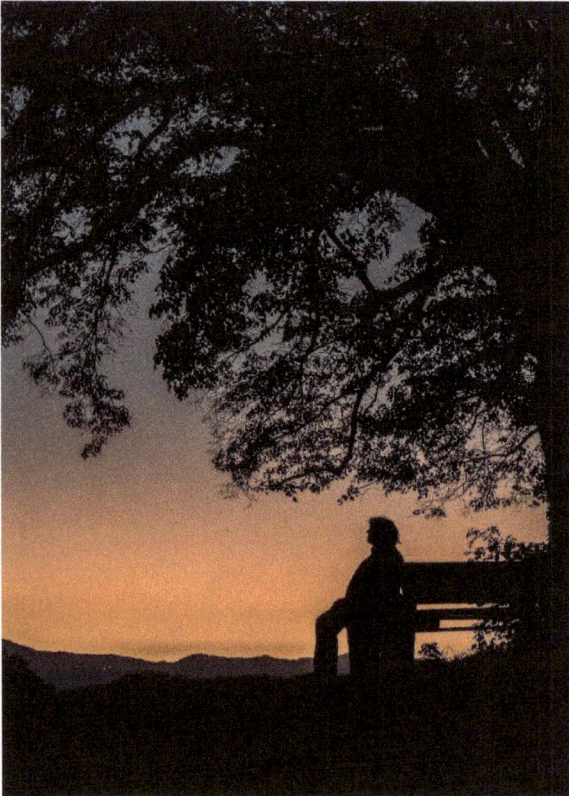

"God's forgiveness
allows us to be honest with ourselves.
We recognize our imperfections,
admit our failures,
and plead to God for clemency."

-- Jonathan Sacks (1948 – 2020)
English Orthodox rabbi, philosopher & author

It is also true that we may endure repeated offenses. We can still forgive. However, the challenges may be greater, and the process could be slower.

The negative behavior could remain ongoing. We often see these patterns of repetition in loving relationships. A repeat offender will try to make the victim feel like a non-person, with less value, and no worth.

The opposite is true. Repeat offenders tend to be extremely insecure people who need to attempt to squash others to feel better about themselves. It takes great strength of character to stand by someone whose apologies and promises collapse repeatedly. Offenders can break hearts, bodies, and spirits, but we must not give up. The human soul will sparkle and shine forever.

"There is no revenge so complete
as forgiveness."

-- Josh Billings (1818 – 1885)
(pen name for Henry Wheeler Shaw)
American humorist

(Photo by Mark Tulin)

3

The Process

First, we get blindsided. Someone that we trusted "did us dirty." They hurt us. The process usually begins with shock and disbelief. That can be haunting.

> *"When a deep injury is done us, we never recover until we forgive."*
>
> -- Alan Paton (1903 – 1983)
> South African author & anti-apartheid activist

(Photo by Darius Bashar)

Then we move into pain. They have truly hurt us. Our heart and soul have been broken. Part of our process is releasing our anger. When we let ourselves feel our pain and resentment, we can also free ourselves from it. Step two is always expressing our anger, hurt, bitterness, and other painful emotions.

"Anger ventilated often hurries towards forgiveness; anger concealed often hardens into revenge."

-- Edward G. Bulwer-Lytton (1803 – 1873)
English writer & politician

(Photo by Valeriia Miller)

I recall sobbing so hard that my chest and stomach heaved up and down. It was uncontrollable. I thought I was losing my mind. How could they have deliberately hurt me as they had?

Letting ourselves feel the hurt is part of processing the pain. No denials will help us forgive.

(Photo by Charlotte Knight)

*"Darkness cannot drive out darkness;
only light can do that.
Hate cannot drive out hate;
only love can do that."*

-- Martin Luther King, Jr. (1929 – 1968)
Baptist minister & social activist

(Photo by Kate Lastella)

Then we can start to heal. Moving on from the pain sets our heart free.

Offenders might do things they may even think are right, at least temporarily. Later, depending on whether or not they grow as a person, they may realize that their choices, words, and behaviors were purely self-serving, self-righteous, or even selfish.

At least they may come to realize that they needlessly and wrongly hurt someone. Then again, we must accept that they may never come to such awareness.

However, they still may try to pretend that their actions, based on negative emotions, like rage or jealousy, were logical and even correct. They fully condone their own stormy misdeeds.

"Forgiveness is an act of the will,
and the will can function
regardless of the temperature of the heart."

-- Corrie Ten Boom (1892 – 1983)
Dutch clockmaker

Seeking a silver lining requires us to be the "bigger people." We take another step in our growth process and try to feel empathy for the one who did us wrong. Even when we disagree whole-heartedly with what they have done, it is tremendously healing to try and understand their motivations.

Perhaps they needed money. Perhaps they needed to feel stronger or smarter or more in control. Perhaps they were taking out their own issues on us. Trying to figure out an offender's reasoning, no matter how lame it may be, empowers us.

> *"Acceptance and tolerance*
> *and forgiveness,*
> *those are life-altering lessons."*

> -- Jessica Lange (1949 -)
> American actress

We will know when we have empathized with an offender and accepted the past as something we cannot change. We may even catch a little smile crossing our face, or we may squelch that surprising giggle. We can find ourselves chuckling to think of the offender's foolishness.

In the end, they are the big losers. We can even wish them well as they carry on in their delusions of righteousness, while we hope they do not continue to hurt others.

"You will know
that forgiveness has begun
when you recall those who hurt you
and feel the power to wish them well."

-- Lewis B. Smedes (1921 – 2002)
American Reformed Christian author,
ethicist & theologian

The action of forgiving includes acknowledging the offense for what it is. We also learn to understand the short- and long-term impact of the offense. Then we can choose to release any feelings of resentment.

Accepting the pain they have caused is vital. It is real. There is nothing to be gained by suppressing or ignoring the pain we feel.

Releasing the pain may involve talking with a trusted person. Or we can write down our feelings and confusions. We could also seek professional guidance. We can take any steps needed to work through this very real process.

*"Every one of us
has been disappointed before
and have had to go
through the grieving process
of anger and disappointment
and then acceptance and forgiveness."*

-- Mathew Knowles (1952 -)
American record executive

(Photo by Trym Nilsen)

We also can try to understand the other person's perspective, no matter how ill-guided they may have been. Even when we do not condone their actions, trying to understand their actions and choices helps us reduce bitterness.

This may sound impossible when we are in the throes of the offense itself. However, it is very satisfying when we are ready.

(Photo by Melanie Stander)

"I learned a long time ago
that some people
would rather die than forgive.
It's a strange truth,
but forgiveness
is a painful and difficult process.
It's not something that happens overnight.
It's an evolution of the heart."

-- Sue Monk Kidd (1948 -)
American author

(Photo by Artem Beliaikin)

We can find "a happy place." We do this by seeking solace in the aspects of life that are positive and peaceful.

I found it. We all can. We may even end up recognizing that had we not been mistreated by that loved one, we would have found ourselves on a very different path than where we were, where we were going, and where we needed to be.

That's one of Life's fabulous twists. We forgive our offender. Then we can find ourselves flourishing in a place we like even better than where we had previously been. Sweet!

(Photo by Mohamed Nohassi)

Just know that the process is a continuing one. We can do this! The sweetest victory is that forgiving sets us free... free from the horrendous weight of the offensive burden.

"Forgiveness takes time.
It is the last step of the grieving process."

-- Elin Nordegren (1980 -)
Swedish model

(Photo by Omar Sotillo)

4

Surviving the Pain

"Genuine forgiveness
does not deny anger
but faces it head-on."

-- Alice Miller (1923 – 2010)
Polish Swiss psychologist & philosopher

To process our pain, we must first let ourselves feel the hurtful emotions. We do not need to try and bury our pain. In fact, we should let ourselves feel passionately distressed. We may even feel hateful toward the wrongdoer. We are angry.

We should let those emotions play out so that we can process them. We need to feel our angst, or that anxiety may get the chance to gobble us up from inside. This would absolutely be unhealthy.

"I can have peace of mind
only when I forgive rather than judge."

-- Gerald G. Jampolsky (1925 – 2020)
American psychiatrist

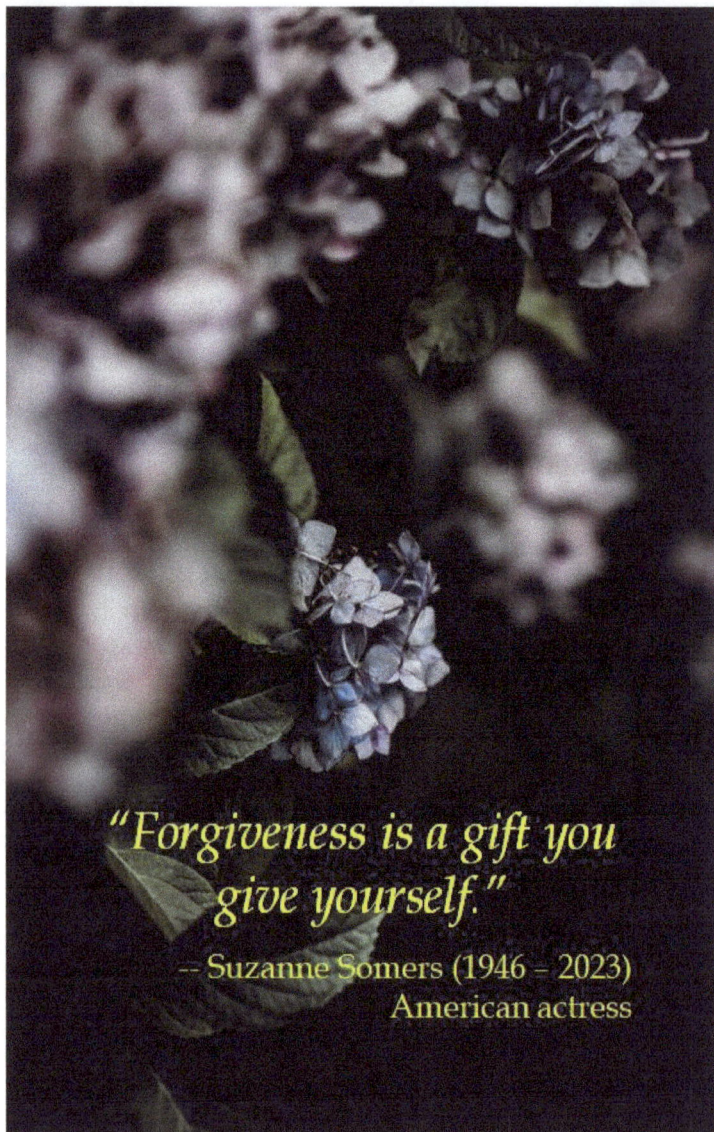

"Forgiveness is a gift you give yourself."

-- Suzanne Somers (1946 – 2023)
American actress

So, take the time to feel the hurt. Cry. Yell. Release it. If we don't, we may never be able to forgive. This is because the painful distress is still balled up inside us.

"If you are bitter,
you are like a dry leaf
that you can just squash,
and you can get blown away by the wind.
There is much more wisdom in forgiveness."

-- Vusi Mahlasela (1965 -)
South African singer-songwriter

Once we have allowed ourselves enough time to feel these emotions, we may be able to start to recognize the harm the offenses committed against us caused. This is where our logical side kicks in and helps us step up from the deep hollows of our heart ache.

"Resentment is like drinking poison and then
hoping it will kill your enemies."

-- Nelson Mandela (1918 – 2013)
South African politician & anti-apartheid activist

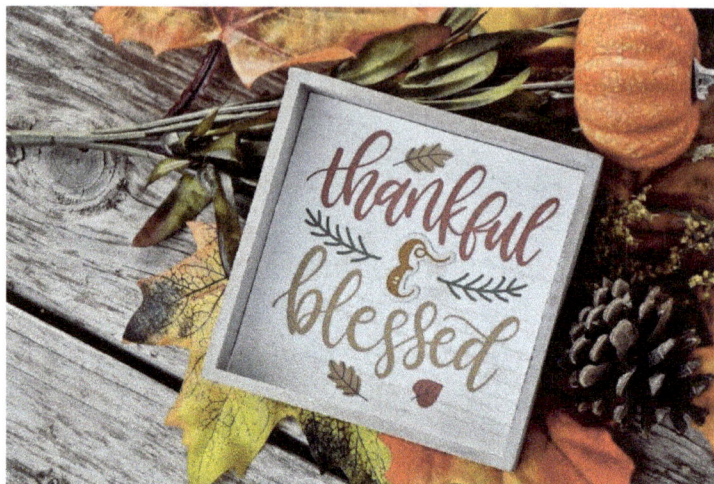

(Photo by Kiy Turk)

It is important to focus on all that we do have for which we should be grateful. This is healthy. We do not want to sink into such a deep, dark hole of despair that we lose sight of all the good around us.

*"Always forgive your enemies –
nothing annoys them so much."*

-- Oscar Wilde (1854 – 1900)
Irish author, poet & playwright

If we find we are unable to see anything good, or we feel stuck in the mud, wallowing in our hurt, we should seek some support. This could be done through a professional counselor. Sometimes, we are fortunate to have a close and trusted friend who can help us find balance and see the worth in ourselves and our world.

> *"Forgiveness is not*
> *to give the other person peace.*
> *Forgiveness is for you.*
> *Take that opportunity."*

-- Mackenzie Phillips (1959 -)
American actress

Remember that embracing compassion cultivates empathy. This is true for both us and the offending person. Most importantly, our bottom line will reflect inner peace and healing.

(Photo by Andrej Lisakov)

5

<u>Deciding to Forgive</u>

"Forgiveness is not a feeling –
it's a decision we make because
we want to do what's right before God.
It's a quality decision that won't be easy
and it may take time to get through the process,
depending on the severity of the offense."

-- Joyce Meyer (1943 -)
American author & speaker

Forgiving is not condoning the wrongdoer or their actions. When we decide to forgive someone, we are choosing to move forward. We are learning to release any deeply held resentment.

"I find forgiveness to be really healthy."

-- Ben Affleck (1972 -)
American actor & filmmaker

Forgiving someone is also good for our overall health. Forgiveness boosts our mental, emotional, and spiritual wellness.

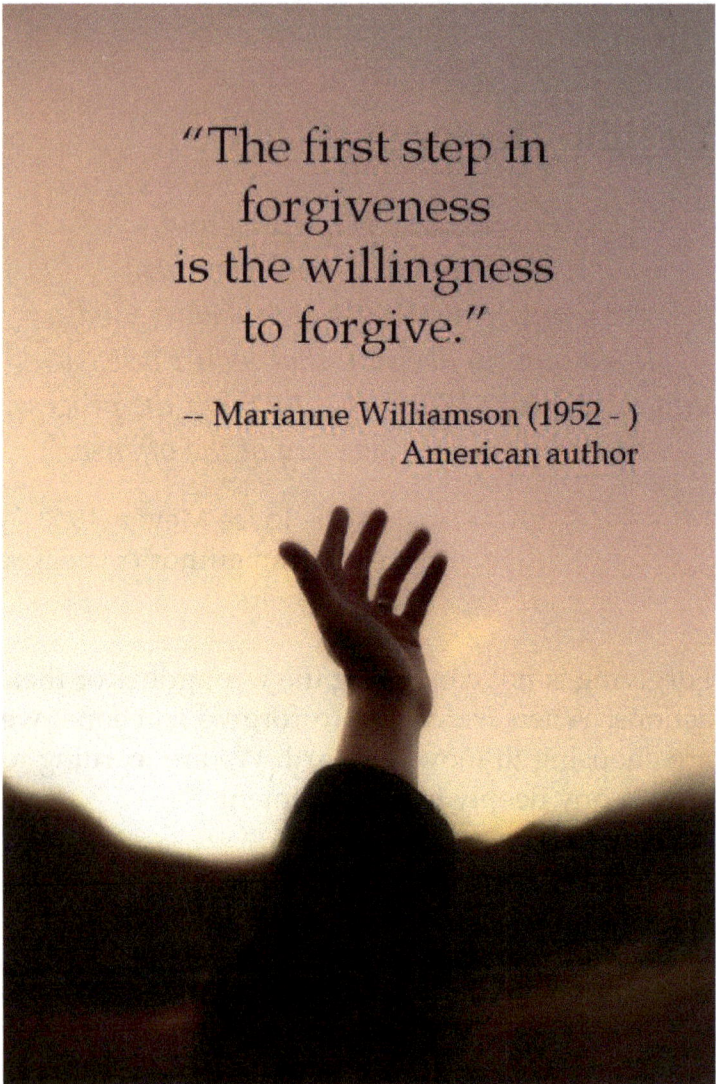

"The first step in
forgiveness
is the willingness
to forgive."

-- Marianne Williamson (1952 -)
American author

(Photo by Joshua Earle)

This also dramatically reduces distress, which is
good for our physical health, too.

We should not expect an easy journey. This is especially true when a wound is highly personal, or the injustice was inflicted by a very close friend, spouse, or family member.

(Photo by Vlad Bagacian)

"It's not an easy journey
to get to a place where you forgive people.
But it is such a powerful place,
because it frees you."

-- Tyler Perry (1969 -)
American actor & filmmaker

We may want to say that we have forgiveness in our heart. And yet, saying it and living it are very different things.

To forgive, we must acknowledge the wrong and the pain. If we then decide to forgive, we can move forward with action steps, such as empathy.

"Forgiveness is not always easy.
At times,
it feels more painful
than the wound we suffered,
to forgive the one that inflicted it.
And yet,
there is no peace without forgiveness."

-- Marianne Williamson (1952 -)
American author

We can empathize with the offender because they may not have realized what they were doing. Sadly, it is also true that they may not have wanted to learn or acknowledge anything new beyond their limited knowledge of the particular situation.

"We all know in our hearts
that forgiveness is the right thing;
it's just a matter of
being inspired to reach that place."

-- Nazanin Boniadi (1980 -)
British actress & activist

(Photo by Nicolas Gaborit)

We've all heard the old adages. "You can lead a horse to water, but you cannot make him drink." "You can't push a rope." "You can't put toothpaste back in the tube." One of my favorites is, "You can't teach a pig to sing. You can try, but you'll just frustrate yourself and annoy the pig."

(Photo by Hans Isaacson)

However, when someone is ill-advised or taking a harsh position that can only hurt us, we have a natural human response. We try and help them see the logic they are missing.

We struggle to understand that they are unable to see reason nor facts that are uncomfortable to them or the scenario and results they seek. They are unable or unwilling to open their brains, and they feel justified in wounding others.

*"It is easier to forgive an enemy
than to forgive a friend."*

-- William Blake (1757 – 1827)
English poet & painter

When we give in and let the offender win, it hurts. The loss hurts, yes. The injury hurts. The worst pain is that a trusted person would knowingly inflict harm on us. Ouch.

So, the decision to forgive takes a deep personal toll. We must consciously decide to let go of negative hard feelings and resentment for someone who has wronged us.

We can expect the road to get bumpier if the offender feigns their choices and actions were good, right, and justified. Still, we can do this.

*"We think that forgiveness is weakness,
but it's absolutely not;
it takes a very strong person to forgive."*

-- T. D. Jakes (1957 -)
American Christian evangelical pastor

(Photo by Getty Images)

Deciding to forgive the seemingly unforgivable unburdens our hearts of the hurts that could otherwise haunt us for a very long time. Forgiving someone enables us to heal and move forward.

We are deciding we want to move forward and let go of the pain. Again, forgiving the offender does not mean we condone their ill deeds. But we do have to muster up all the empathy and compassion we possibly can.

(Photo by Beyza Yurtkuran)

*"There is freedom in forgiveness,
and it's not that hard to do
once you get into the habit."*

-- Dana Perino (1972 -)
Commentator, news anchor, &
former White House press secretary

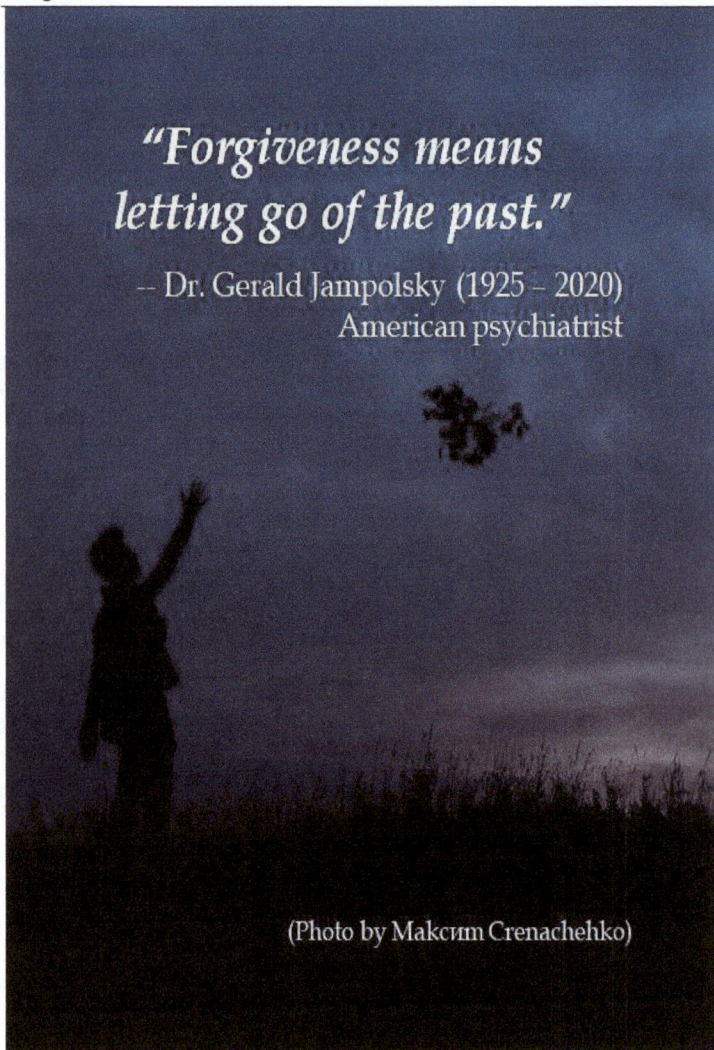

"Forgiveness means letting go of the past."

-- Dr. Gerald Jampolsky (1925 – 2020)
American psychiatrist

(Photo by Максим Crenachehko)

6

Letting Go

The old expression says, "Let go and let God." It sounds so simple in theory, and yet in practice it can be far more challenging.

> *"The weak can never forgive.*
> *Forgiveness is the attribute of the strong."*

-- Mahatma Gandhi (1869 – 1948)
Indian lawyer & political ethicist

We cannot simply snap our fingers and lose any and all ill feelings toward the person who wreaked havoc in our life. We can, however, gradually release ourselves from even thinking about the situation.

Naturally, the thoughts return when we are reminded. However, the angst these thoughts bring can be lessened over time.

Whether we like it or not, a bit or a lot of resentment will likely gnaw at our hearts that this person would ever knowingly do what they have done.

"Never does the human soul
appear so strong
as when it foregoes revenge
and dares to forgive an injury."

-- Edwin Hubbel Chapin (1814 – 1880)
American preacher, poet & editor

(Photo by Getty Images)

We can let that resentment go. This requires us to utilize every bit of empathy to try to understand why they were able to do what they did.

No one said this would be easy, but letting go of any resentment is essential. The freedom we feel when we succeed at this is beyond liberating.

(Photo by Getty Images)

"Without forgiveness
life is governed by
an endless cycle of
resentment and retaliation."

-- Roberto Assagioli (1888 – 1974)
Italian psychiatrist & humanistic psychology
pioneer

When a friend betrays our confidence, we can choose to forgive them. We can rebuild the relationship through reconciliation. However, we may be far more cautious in the future.

We can also forgive, wish the ill-doer well, and choose to no longer participate in "their world" or include them in ours. That is fine.

As long as we have forgiven them in our heart, they are free to go about their lives, just as we are. However, we do not have to continue associating with them.

"The bitterest tears
shed over graves
are for words left unsaid
and deeds left undone."

-- Harriet Beecher Stowe (1811 – 1896)
American author & abolitionist

(Photo by Isadore Decamon)

If we do not forgive, it is likely that we are still holding a grudge against the person who hurt us. The Bible teaches us that if we hold something against another person, we are unforgiving. We let it go when we forgive.

However, forgiveness is not simply setting aside or accepting what happened to us. It's not just about ceasing to feel hurt or angry or betrayed.

(Photo by Jamet Lene)

"Forgiveness is a funny thing.
It warms the heart and cools the sting."

-- William Arthur Ward (1921 – 1994)
American writer

Forgiveness requires us to willfully set aside feelings of resentment toward the offender. This can be particularly challenging when someone has been knowingly hurtful, unfair, or has not shown the slightest remorse at having wounded or betrayed us.

(Photo by Priscilla du Preez)

Forgiving someone who hurt us lets us release the emotional control and power that the offender held over us. A betrayer does not need to deserve our forgiveness but forgiving them sets us free.

*"I think the first step
is to understand that forgiveness
does not exonerate the perpetrator.
Forgiveness liberates the victim.
It's a gift you give yourself."*

-- T. D. Jakes (1957 -)
American Christian evangelical pastor

7

And Forget?

Forgiveness does not mean forgetting. Nor does it mean condoning the offense. It's about us releasing negative emotions associated with the offense and the offender.

Repentance would help the wrongdoer. However, that is their responsibility, not ours.

*"Forgive your enemies
but never forget their names."*

-- John F. Kennedy (1917 – 1963)
American politician &
35th President of the United States

We cannot change whatever it is that happened. The affront is in the past. It is done. We are unlikely to be able to totally forget that a trusted person did this to us. However, they do not get to decide what happens next. We do.

"What is forgiven is usually well remembered."

-- Louis Dudek (1918 – 2001)
Canadian poet & academic

(Photo by Kraken Images)

We may choose to rebuild trust. If we want to restore the relationship, reconciliation may not be easy. This will require establishing healthy boundaries to protect ourselves and prevent future issues. We may want to create new patterns for interaction with this person in the future.

"Forgiveness is a virtue of the brave."

-- Indira Gandhi (1917 – 1984)
Indian politician & statesmen
Former Prime Minister of India

Whatever we choose, we are in a time for personal growth and new opportunities We move forward. We grow stronger. We become braver.

"The stupid neither forgive nor forget;
the naive forgive and forget;
the wise forgive but do not forget."

-- Thomas Szasz (1920 – 2012)
Hungarian American academic & psychiatrist

Canceling our awareness of the entire episode is simply not necessary. However, to move onward, we do need to learn how to "let it go."

If we cannot stop experiencing negative distress and stress, it can be a sign of Post-Traumatic Stress Disorder (PTSD). One does not have to have served in a war zone or as a first responder to suffer such risk.

"The only thing I've settled in my mind is that I want to forgive, and forgiveness comes with forgetting."

-- Ingrid Betancourt (1961 -)
Colombian French politician & anti-corruption activist

(Photo by Getty Images)

Keep in mind that reconciliation is not required to forgive someone. We do not have to accept the harmful behavior as okay or acceptable. Nor do we have to restore the original relationship. It is often healthier not to do so.

If someone wrongs us once, it could be an isolated incident. Sad to say, however, this could be part of a systematic pattern. If so, we are hard-pressed to prevent it from happening again.

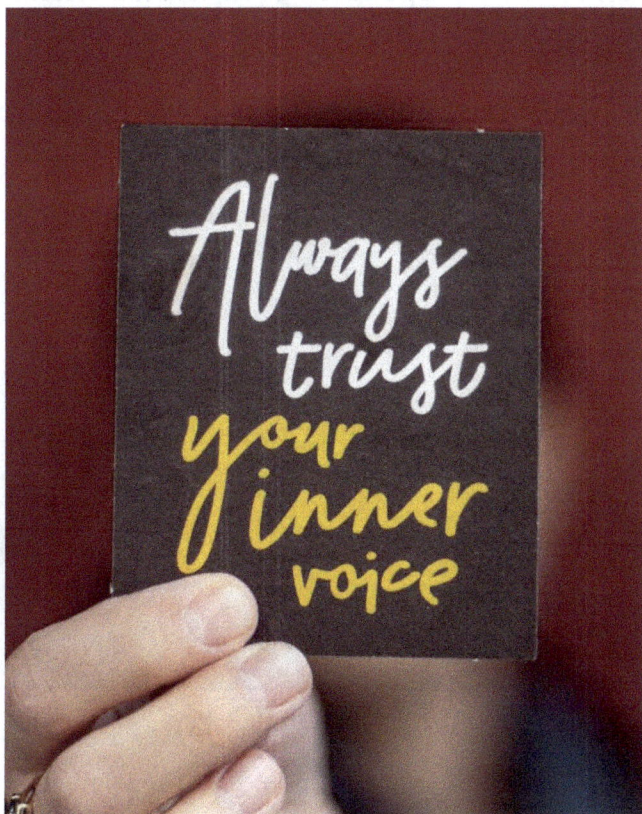

(Photo by Giu Vicente)

"Forgotten is forgiven."

-- F. Scott Fitzgerald (1896 – 1940)
American novelist & essayist

We may forget. We may not. The bottom line is that there is no requirement or need to forgive and forget. Trying to forget a grievous wrong, especially one perpetrated by a trusted friend or family member, is almost impossible.

But when we forgive, we prevent it from consuming us. We can move on with our lives.

<u>Apologies</u>

"Sweet mercy is nobility's true badge."

-- William Shakespeare (1564 – 1616)
English playwright, poet & actor

Some people proudly say, "I make no apologies." I am the opposite. I try to apologize regularly. Why? For example, I am outspoken. I never know when I may have insulted someone else's sensibilities or hurt their feelings. That is never my intention. So, I apologize if I think I may have wounded someone.

"A stiff apology is a second insult...
The injured party does not want to be
compensated because he has been wronged;
he wants to be healed
because he has been hurt."

-- Gilbert K. Chesterton (1874 – 1936)
English author, philosopher & journalist

Even if they don't say it out loud, we can sometimes catch a glance or a look on someone's face. We can get a sense that they may feel some affront.

When we apologize, we open the door to healing conversation. Of course, our apologies must be genuine, or they are a mere dribble.

"Reversing your treatment
of the man you have wronged
is better than asking his forgiveness."

-- Elbert Hubbard (1856 – 1915)
American writer, publisher & philosopher

(Photo by Brett Jordan)

A sincere apology can be the sweetest sound we can make or hear. These are expressions of remorse for hurting someone or betraying them or insulting them or letting them down.

We all want to be rightfully known as someone whose word is good and true. We do not want to hurt others. We certainly do not want to emotionally or physically wound someone we love.

> *"Asking for forgiveness*
> *is just one of the*
> *most painful kind of experiences."*

> -- Nick Nolte (1941 -)
> American actor

Unfortunately, hurts happen. If we caused the pain in any way, we need to apologize to those we injured. We can heartfully let them know the depth of our remorse at harming them or their feelings, betraying their confidence, or harming them in any other way.

"I'm sorry. I am truly sorry."

These appear to be very simple words. We can say a great deal without great complication or pontification.

Apologies express our heartfelt regret at having hurt someone. We do not like letting people down.

"I think when you're happy,
emotions are right near the top.
Mine definitely are. I cry easily, I laugh easily,
I lose my temper easily...
and I beg for forgiveness easily."

-- Nell Carter (1948 – 2003)
American actress & singer

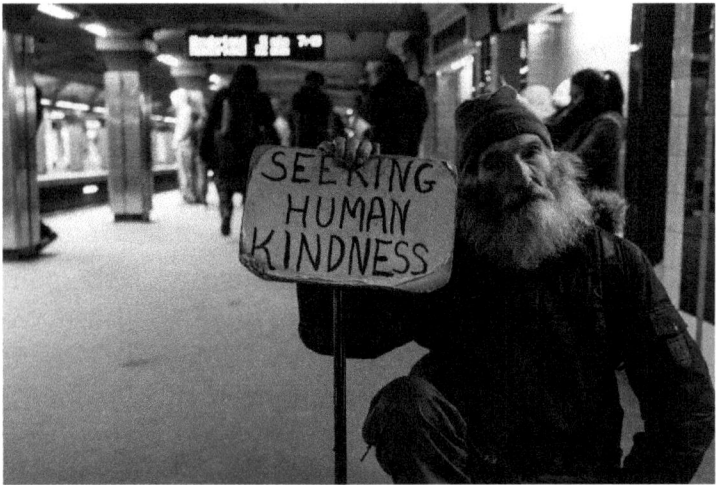

(Photo by Matt Collamer)

Sometimes there is nothing that can be done to undo the harm or rectify the damage. We can still take responsibility for our words or actions and the harm we caused or instigated.

Apologizing requires being a bigger person than we sometimes may have thought we could be. This fact is what occasionally prevents someone from stepping up and even admitting they have caused damage.

(Photo by Matt Reiter)

"Delusion and denial do not equal an apology."

-- Carole Radziwill (1963 -)
American journalist & author

Interestingly, we do not always have to apologize in order to be forgiven. The person we hurt may have a huge heart and forgave us. They may even have done this before we were even aware we had inadvertently injured them. They may forgive us even when our misplaced sensibilities prevent us from recognizing our role in their angst.

Apologizing is a very good thing. It never hurts us to apologize. Well, it might trigger a pang of guilt, especially if we cause harm unknowingly. But sincerely sharing our apology is good for the giver and receiver.

(Photo by Gabriel Ponton)

"When an apology is truly genuine,
all you want in return is forgiveness."

-- Tom Sandoval (1982 -)
American TV personality

For a simple example, I sincerely apologize if words I have shared have offended anyone. I write directly from my heart, as if we were chatting together.

It's obviously not far-fetched to recognize that I may easily have made an off-the-cuff or even well-thought-out statement that someone else may have taken quite personally and felt hurt. As someone who wishes to not harm others, I sincerely apologize.

(Photo by Andrew Petrischev)

"Right actions in the future
are the best apologies
for bad actions in the past."

-- Tryon Edwards (1809 – 1894)
American Congregational theologian

(Photo by Inna Gurina)

9

<u>Self-Forgiveness</u>

"To forgive is to set a prisoner free
and discover that the prisoner was you."

-- Lewis B. Smedes (1921 – 2002)
American Christian Reformed author
& theologian

Self-forgiveness is vital because we are all humans. We are imperfect. We all make mistakes. Knowingly or unknowingly, we hurt other people. We do them wrong.

"Mistakes are always forgivable,
if one has the courage to admit them."

-- Bruce Lee (1940 – 1973)
Hong Kong American martial artist & actor

These may be large or small affronts. Regardless, we need to forgive ourselves. We all have shortcomings.

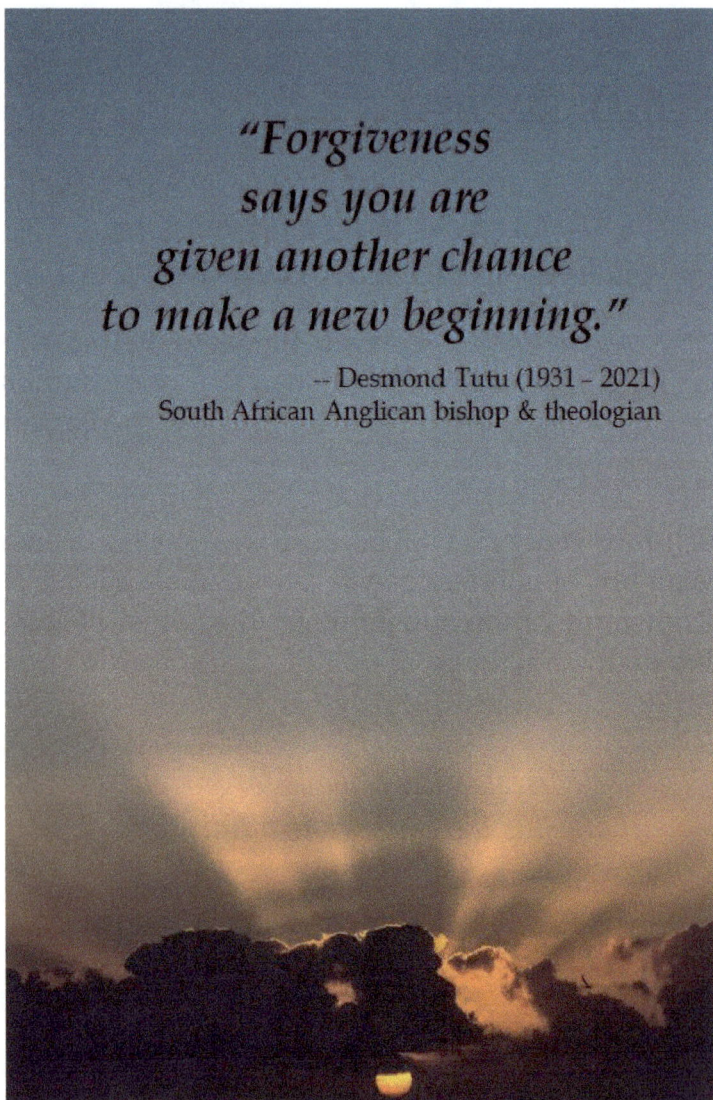

*"Forgiveness
says you are
given another chance
to make a new beginning."*

-- Desmond Tutu (1931 – 2021)
South African Anglican bishop & theologian

(Photo by Klanarong Chitmung)

"Forgive me my nonsense,
as I also forgive the nonsense
of those that think they talk sense."

-- Robert Frost (1874 – 1963)
American poet

As adults, we sometimes find ourselves in a vicious cycle. Someone does us wrong. We forgive them. Then they do us wrong again. And we forgive them again.

Even if they have apologized and sounded sincere, they continue to be bad actors. And we continue to let it happen. We must learn to forgive ourselves.

"It is in pardoning that we are pardoned."

-- St. Francis of Assisi (1181 – 1224)
(Giovanni di Petro de Bernardone)
Italian mystic, poet & Catholic friar
Founder of Franciscans religious order

(Photo by Jon Tyson)

"As we know, forgiveness of oneself is the hardest of all the forgivenesses."

-- Joan Baez (1941 -)
American folk singer & social activist

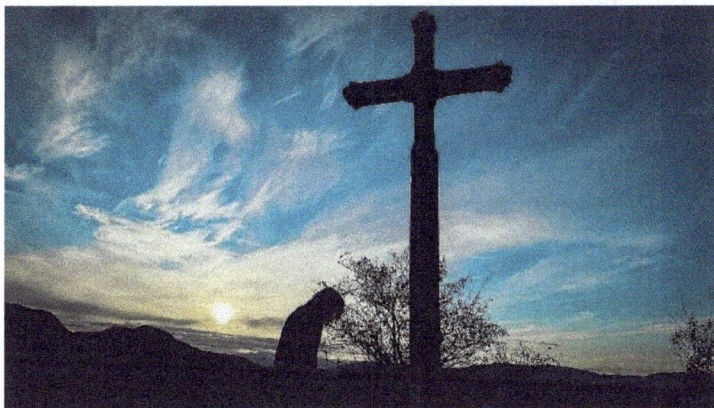

(Photo by Jamet Lene)

"Many times,
the decisions we make
affect and hurt your closest friends
and family the most.
I have a lot of regrets in that regard.
But God has forgiven me,
which I am very thankful for.
It has enabled me to forgive myself
and move forward one day at a time."

-- Lex Luger (1958 -)
American wrestler, body builder
& football player

Do we love too much? Are we too insecure? Do we totally lack the self-esteem and courage to stand up for ourselves and say, "Enough is enough?"

I do not know. I do know that while we grow as people, we need to forgive ourselves. We are mere mortals.

"How unhappy
is he who cannot forgive himself."

-- Publilius Syrus (85 BC – 43 BC)
Latin writer
Brought as a slave to Roman Italy

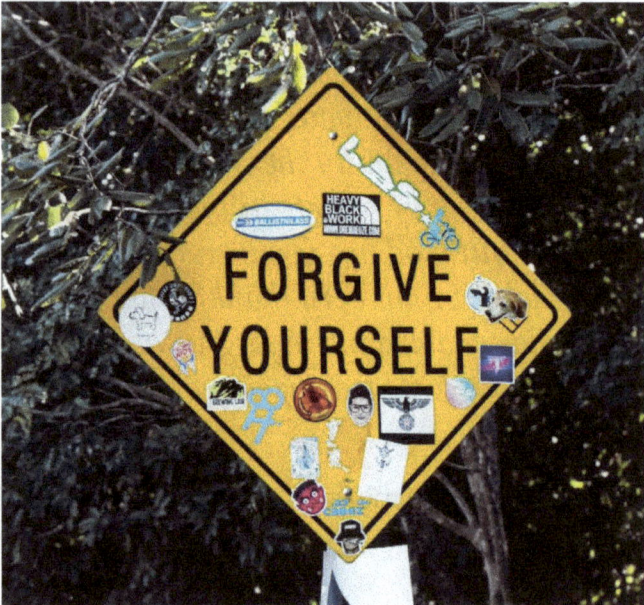

(Photo by Simon Humler)

Like this entire forgiveness process, learning how to give ourselves a break is not easy. Friends may criticize us for stepping right back into harm's way… again.

Take comfort by trying to remember that we are developing good living skills. This takes time. However, teaching ourselves to forgive ourselves is always worthwhile.

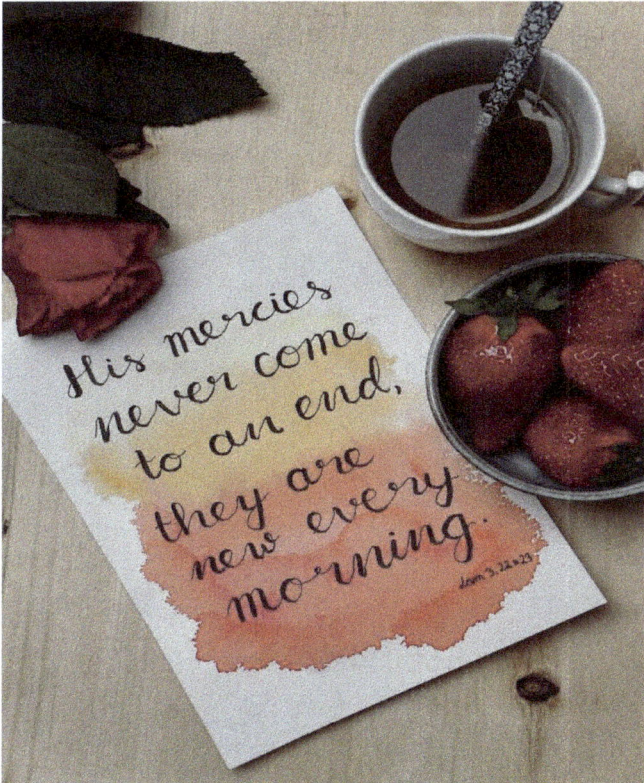

His mercies never come to an end, they are new every morning.

(Photo by Miriam Gee)

*"God may forgive your sins,
but your nervous system won't."*

-- Alfred Korzybski (1879 – 1950)
Polish American philosopher & scholar

Forgiving ourselves requires self-compassion. Only when we forgive ourselves can we move forward.

(Photo by Nader Ayman)

*"Forgive yourself
for your faults and your mistakes
and move on."*

-- Les Brown (1912 – 2001)
American jazz musician

10

In Closing

Always remember that forgiveness is not a sign of weakness. Quite the opposite is true. Forgiveness requires powerful fortitude, remarkable bravery, and deep compassion.

> *"Only the brave know how to forgive...*
> *a coward never forgave;*
> *it is not in his nature."*

-- Laurence Sterne (1713 – 1768)
Irish novelist

Someone may angrily spout off that they want to punch the offender. Well, that is merely an emotional reaction. Such outbursts do not reflect any sort of thoughtful response.

They express the pain and anger that are rightfully part of the process. However, such feelings must be felt, positively examined, and released, or no good can come of them.

(Photo by Mayur Gala)

*"We must develop
and maintain the capacity to forgive.
He who is devoid of the power to forgive
is devoid of the power to love.
There is some good in the worst of us
and some evil in the best of us.
When we discover this,
we are less prone to hate our enemies."*

-- Martin Luther King, Jr. (1929 – 1968)
Baptist minister & social activist

When we go through the process to forgive, we are demonstrating great strength and resilience. It literally takes courage to forgive.

We must confront some monstrously huge and painful emotions. We often must step away from a formerly trusted person and let them go from our lives.

*"The practice of forgiveness
is our most important contribution
to the healing of the world."*

-- Marianne Williamson (1952 -)
American author

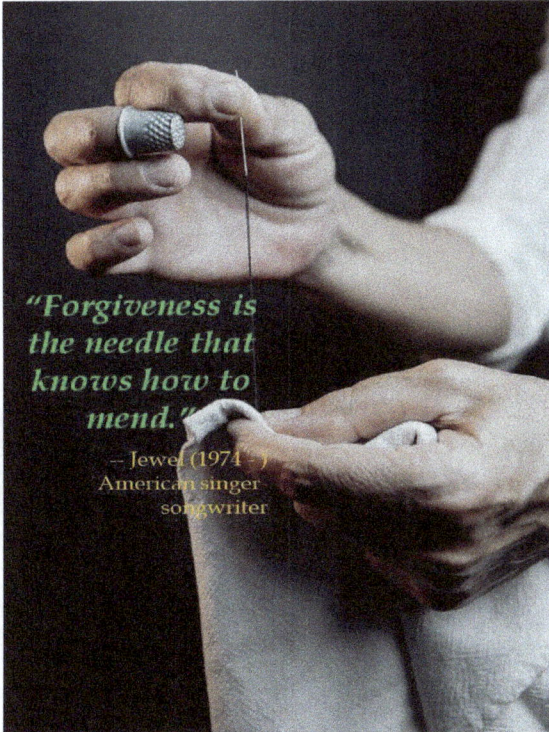

"Forgiveness is the needle that knows how to mend."

-- Jewel (1974 -)
American singer
songwriter

Forgiving also improves our mental health. Stress is reduced, which is always a constructive, healthy choice. Forgiveness promotes our overall well-being and positive state of mind.

"A mistake is always forgivable,
rarely excusable
and always unacceptable."

-- Robert Fripp (1946 -)
English musician, composer & record producer
Founder & guitarist of King Crimson

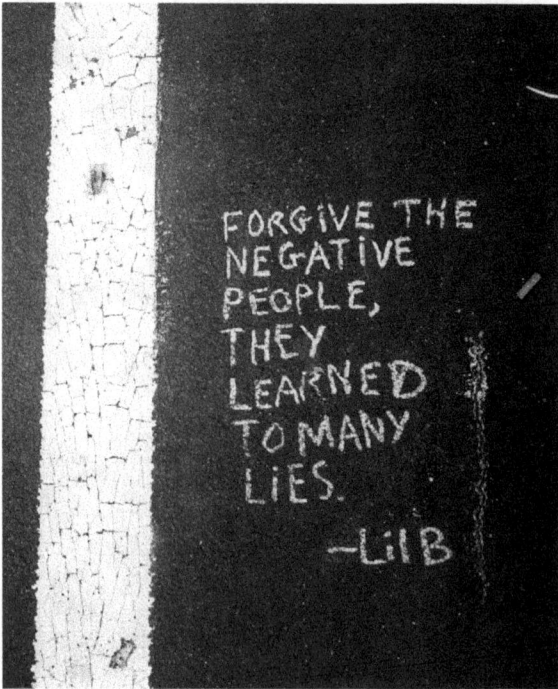

(Photo by Susan Yin)

Photography Credits

Thank you to everyone who entrusted me with the use of their beautiful photographs.

Nader Ayman
Vlad Bagacian
Danila Balashkin
Darius Bashar
Artem Beliaikin
Natalia Blauth
Ave Calvar
Klanarong Chitmung
Matt Collamer
Makevm Crenachehko
Isadore Decamon
Priscilla du Preez
Joshua Earle
Semenay Erdogan
Stacey Franco
Nicolas Gaborit
Mayur Gala
Miriam Gee
Inna Gurina
Simon Humler
Getty Images
Kraken Images
Hans Isaacson
Brett Jordan
Charlotte Knight
Kate Lastella

Jamet Lene
Andrej Lisakov
Valeriia Miller
Daniel Mirlea
Pablo Merchán Montes
Adrien Moureaux
Trym Nilsen
Mohamed Nohassi
Andrew Petrischev
Johannes Plenio
Gabriel Ponton
Matt Reiter
Juan Pablo Rodriguez
Shah Rokh
Mathew Schwartz
Alex Shute
Omar Sotillo
Annie Spratt
Melanie Stander
Mark Tulin
Kiy Turk
Jon Tyson
Giu Vincente
Susan Yin
Beyza Yurtkuran

Special thanks to Junior Reis for the cover photo.

(Photo by Junior Reis)

About the Author

Cathy Burnham Martin's first published work came in elementary school when an early poem won a town library contest. That was back when her parents refused to let her have the then-popular "Chatty Cathy" doll, stating that one chatty Cathy in the house was more than enough. Though poetry took a back seat, she drove her writing and blabbing proficiencies along a highly eclectic career path through college recruitment, telecom marketing, corporate communications, TV broadcasting with an ABC affiliate, station management of an award-winning PEG-access station, bank organizing, and investor relations. An active board member and volunteer, she received Easter Seals' David P. Goodwin Lifetime Commitment Award. This professional voiceover artist, humorist, musical actress, journalist, and dedicated foodie earned numerous awards as a news anchor and businesswoman. She has produced and hosted groundbreaking documentaries, TV specials, and news reports, from the Moscow Superpower Summit and the opening of the Berlin Wall to coverage of Presidential Primaries. A born storyteller and business speaker dubbed "The Morale Booster," Cathy is a member of Actors Equity and writes daily articles for social media and the GoodLiving123.com website.

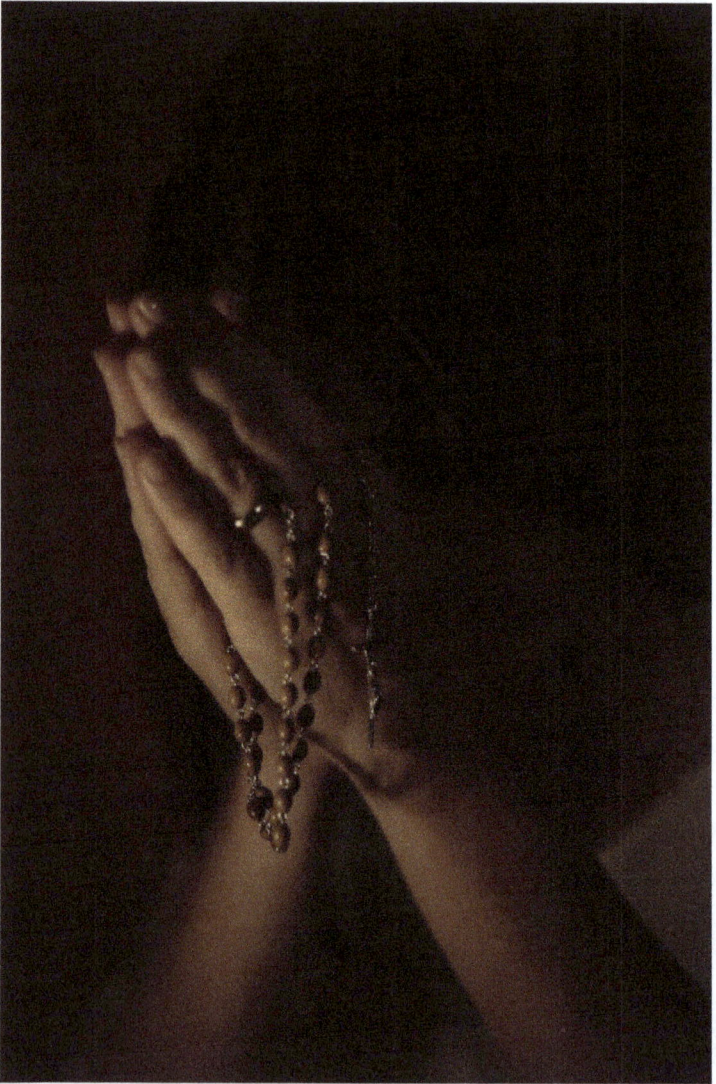

(Photo by Getty Images)

Other Titles

Life Seasonings series:
  Perspectives
  Hope
  Happiness

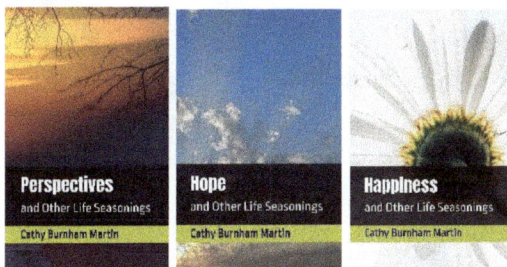

The Destiny trilogy:
  Destiny of Dreams… Time Is Dear
  Destiny of Determination… Faith and Family
  Destiny of Daring… Never Forget

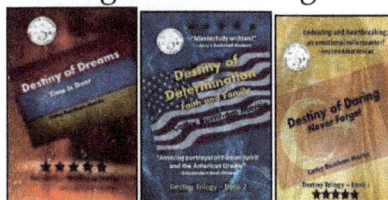

A Dangerous Book for Dogs:
  Train Your Humans with the Bandit Method
Dog Days in the Life of the Miles-Mannered Man

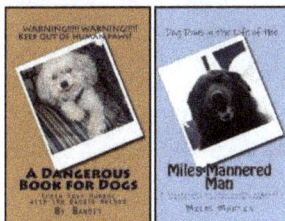

Healthy Thinking Habits:
    Seven Attitude Skills Simplified
Good Living Skills: Learned from My Mother
Encouragement: How to Be and Find Your Best

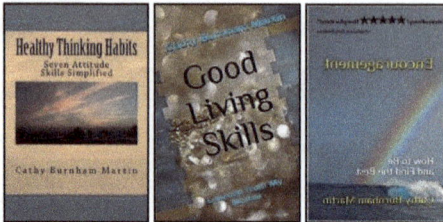

Of the Same Blood: Your Eurasian Heritage
The Ronald...
    Daydreams, Wonderments & Other Ponderings

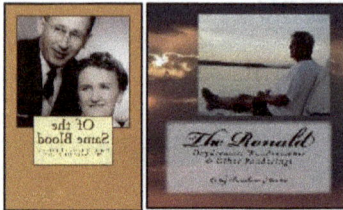

The Bimbo Has Brains... and Other Freaky Facts
The Bimbo Has MORE Brains...
    Surviving Political Correctness

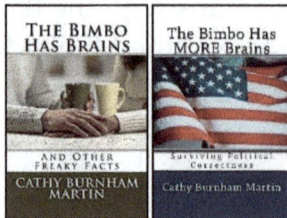

From the KISS Keep It Super Simple cookbooks:

50 Years of Fabulous Family Favorites
   Sippers, Starters, and Sweets
   Lunch, Brunch, and Entrees
   Sides, Soup, Salad, Snacks, Etc.

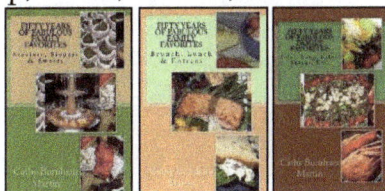

Champagne! Facts, Fizz, Food, & Fun
Cranberry Cooking

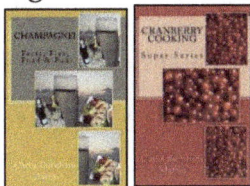

Dockside Dining: (series)
   Round One
   A Second Helping
   Back for Thirds

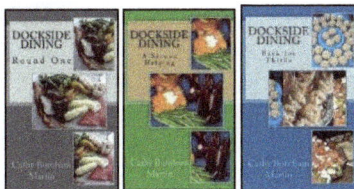

Lobacious Lobster...
   Decadently Super Simple Recipes

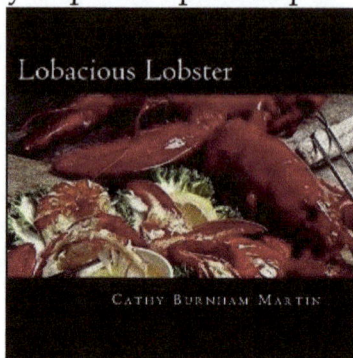

Find all books by Cathy Burnham Martin
in paperback, digital, and audiobook
formats anywhere books are sold and on
her **www.GoodLiving123.com** site.

Partial List of Audiobooks Narrated by Cathy Burnham Martin

Fiction

Destiny Trilogy:
    Destiny of Dreams... Time Is Dear
      (Violent content warning)
    Destiny of Determination... Faith and Family
    Destiny of Daring... Never Forget
A Dangerous Book for Dogs...
    Train Your Humans with the Bandit Method
Kremlins Trilogy (Violent content warning)
    Citadels of Fire
    Bastions of Blood
    Dungeons of Destiny:
        An Epic Russian Historical Romance
Daniel's Fork: A Mystery Set in the
      Daniel's Fork Universe
        (Adult content warning)
The Relentless Brit

Non-Fiction

Encouragement: How to Be and Find the Best
Good Living Skills... Learned from My Mother
Healthy Thinking Habits:
    Seven Attitude Skills Simplified
The Bimbo Has Brains: And Other Freaky Facts
The Bimbo Has MORE Brains:
    Surviving Political Correctness
31 Days to a Stronger Marriage:
    A Guide to Building Closer Relationships
Exploring Past Lives: A Guide to the Soul's Travels
Why We Fail in Love: A Study into the Pursuit of
    One of Mankind's Most Precious Desires
The Hormone Fix: Naturally Rebalance Your System
    in 10 Weeks

www.ingramcontent.com/pod-product-compliance
Lightning Source LLC
Chambersburg PA
CBHW060400050426
42449CB00009B/1838